Dimpled

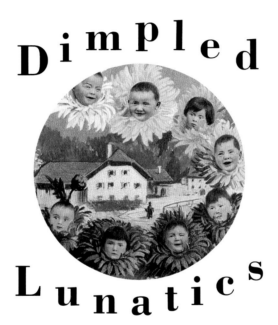

Lunatics

Dimpled

Lunatics

Suzanne Slesin, Emily Gwathmey, and John Margolies

Design by Adriane Stark

Clarkson Potter/Publishers • New York

THANK YOU: Andreas Brown at the Gotham Book Mart in New York; our agents, Lucy Kroll and Barbara Hogenson; our editor, Roy Finamore; Howard Klein and Adriane Stark; Kristen Behrens; and Peter Ustinov for the title to Chapter 2.

To our babies: Jake and Lucie Steinberg; Annie Gwathmey; and Lucille and Fidi.

Copyright © 1993 by Suzanne Slesin, Emily Gwathmey, and John Margolies

Published by Clarkson Potter/Publishers, 201 East 50th Street, New York, New York 10022. Member of the Crown Publishing Group.
Random House, Inc. New York, Toronto, London, Sydney, Auckland
CLARKSON N. POTTER, POTTER, and colophon are trademarks of Clarkson N. Potter, Inc.

Manufactured in Hong Kong.

Library of Congress Cataloging-in-Publication Data

Slesin, Suzanne.
   Dimpled lunatics : the mad world of babyhood / Suzanne Slesin, Emily Gwathmey, and John Margolies ; design by Adriane Stark.
   1. Children —Quotations. 2.Babies—Humor.   I. Gwathmey, Emily Margolin. II.   Margolies, John. III. Title.
PN6084.C5S54   1993
305.23—dc20   92-8966
                                        CIP

ISBN 0-517-58932-X
10 9 8 7 6 5 4 3 2 1
First Edition

Contents

A

child is

a curly, dimpled

lunatic.

—Ralph Waldo

Emerson

Introduction

Who could ever resist babies? At the turn of the century, the more "dimpled lunatics" bouncing around the house, the merrier, and a large family was a sign of fecundity and prosperity. Sure, there might be more mouths to feed, but there were more lovely little things to love—and more hands to help out with chores in the house or work in the fields.

What are these Babies after?

Big families were something to be wished for. That might explain the popularity of the Victorian postcards that depicted dozens of cute "little people" in imaginary scenes. "Fantasy babies"—as these postcards were known—were a popular subject in an era when millions of postcards were produced and sent, in much the same way we would make telephone calls today.

The postcards themselves were sophisticated works of art, produced by elaborate technical printing processes that did justice to the images themselves: amusing, perplexing, and entertaining tableaux that placed babies and small children in countless situations that suggest the Surrealists' vision, long before that particular art movement came into being.

Many of the "fantasy baby" postcards illustrated the eternal question: "Where do the little darlings come from anyway?" In the realm of prim Victorian morality, biological realities were not deemed appropriate for publication—on postcards or anywhere else. Instead myths and legends abounded. Babies were airlifted by dirigible or stork, hatched in the henhouse, and fished from the river.

English babies were delivered by the postman and French tots were found in the cabbage patch (*mais oui, mon petit chou*). And in this world, babies—frequently masquerading as miniature grownups—reign supreme.

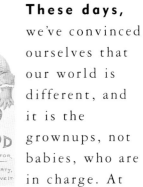

These days, we've convinced ourselves that our world is different, and it is the grownups, not babies, who are in charge. At least, that is, until the midnight hour when we come face-to-face with that adorable, howling bundle of joy, who has taken over our lives in much the same way his legions of mischievous cohorts filled the Victorian dreamscape.

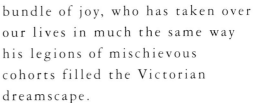

W h e r e   D o   B a b i e s   C o m e   F r o m ?

Congratulations. We all knew you had it in you. —Dorothy Parker

Where did you come

from, baby dear?

Out of the

Everywhere, into

the here.

—George MacDonald

Q. Where did I come from?

A. The postman brought you,

by special delivery.

Q. Where did I come from?

A. The cabbage patch,

mon petit chou.

Q. Where did I come from?

A. The stork came, dropped

you down the chimney, and

bit my foot so I could stay in bed

and take care of you.

Q. Where did I come from?

A. A hollow tree.

Q. Where did I come from?

A. The center of the earth.

L'AÉROPLANE
DU
BONHEUR

If men had
to have babies,
they would
only have
one each.
—Diana, Princess
of Wales

My mother
groan'd, my
father wept,
Into the
dangerous world
I leapt;
Helpless, naked,
piping loud,
Like a fiend hid
in a cloud.
—William Blake

There's only one pretty child

in the world and every mother has it. —Proverb

FUDGE, FUDGE,

tell the judge.
Mama's got a
newborn baby. It
isn't a girl and it
isn't a boy, It's
just a fair young
lady. Wrap it up in
tissue paper And
send it up the
elevator. First
floor, miss. Second
floor, miss. Third
floor, miss. Fourth
floor, Kick it out
the elevator door!
—Skip-rope rhyme

The trouble with children is that they

are not returnable. —Quentin Crisp

THE BONES ON WHICH CHILDREN
SHARPEN THEIR TEETH

Worthy Parents

réjoui   *résigné*   *désespéré*

There was a young girl who begat

Three brats by name

Nat, Pat, and Tat.

It was fun in the breeding

But hell in the feeding,

When she found there

was no tit for Tat. —Anonymous

One of the most visible effects of a child's presence in the household is to turn the worthy parents into complete idiots when without him, they would perhaps have remained mere imbeciles. —George Courteline

IN THE BEGINNING

WOMAN GAVE MAN

AN

NOW SHE GIVES HIM

A

Children

aren't happy

with nothing

to ignore,

And that's

what parents

were created

for.

—Ogden Nash

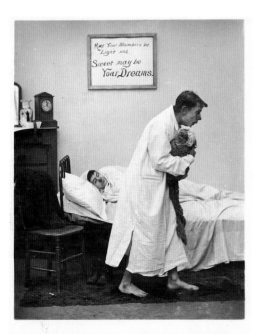

CAKE WALK UP-TO-DATE.

MY HUSBAND and I are either going to buy a dog or have a child. We can't decide whether to ruin our carpet or ruin our lives. —Rita Rudner

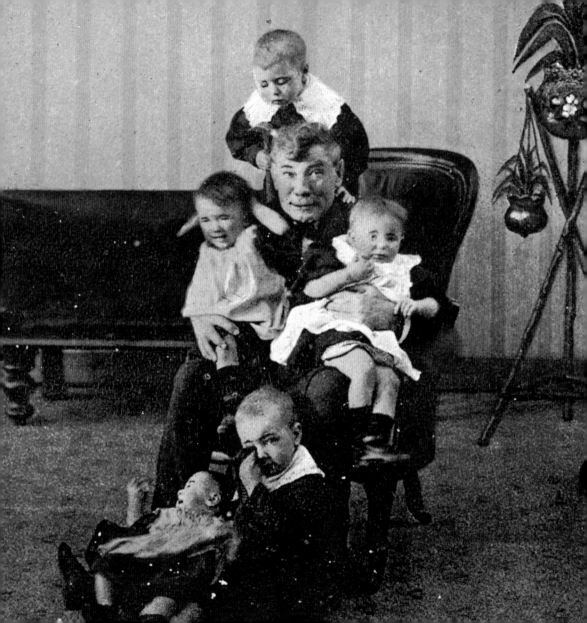

Bringing Up Baby

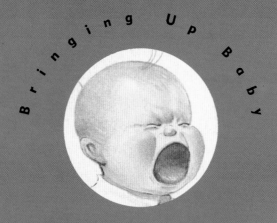

My wife and I just had a baby, and there's nothing relaxed about them. They're like these little tense things who scream in order to fall asleep. Just like adults, only more direct. - Ian Shoales

I love children—especially when they cry, for then someone takes them away. —Nancy Mitford

THEY CRY

Things have

been kinda

squally.

—Old postcard

A. HIGH BAWL

COPYRIGHT 1906 BY BAMFORTH & CO

CURDS AND WHEY

2 pints milk

1 teaspoon junket

Heat the milk to 86 degrees.
Remove the pot from the heat
and stir in the junket.
Pour the mixture into small ramekins
and let cool for two hours.
Stir to separate the curds from the whey.
Sprinkle with sugar.

This would be a better world for children if parents had to eat the spinach. — Groucho Marx

COD LIVER OIL

He will soon learn to like it.

When he has learned to take

the oil willingly, his cheeks

will not have to be held.

—*Dr. Herman N. Bundesen*

He knows a good thing when he sees it!

A DRINK OF WATER

should be given to the baby each day. This is a necessity, yet there are many infants who never receive it, simply because they are unable to ask for it.

—*The Delineator* magazine

There are times when parenthood seems nothing but feeding the mouth that bites you. — Peter de Vries

THEY GO POTTY

Why does your brother hide under the bed? Because he

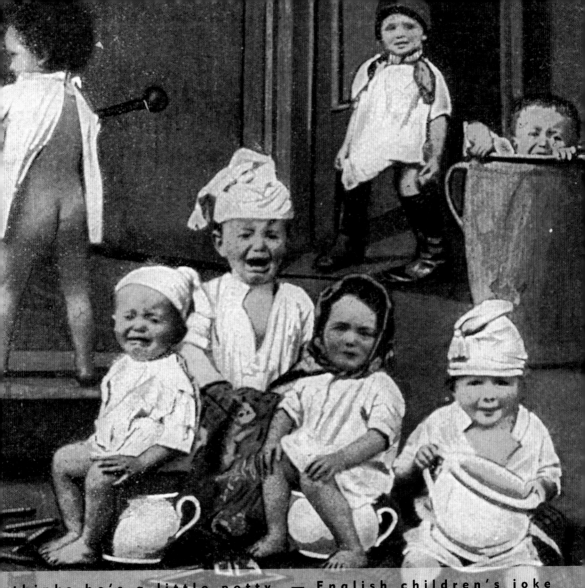

thinks he's a little potty. — English children's joke

A baby is an alimentary canal with a loud voice at one

Labor.

Capital.

end and no responsibility at the other. — E. Adamson

I once knew a chap who
had a system of just
hanging the baby on the

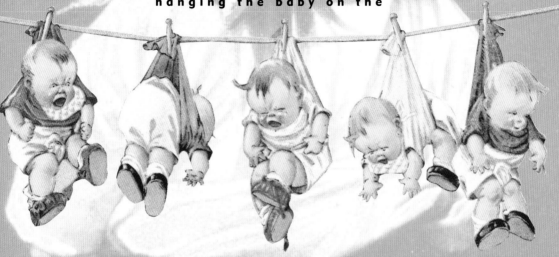

clothesline to dry and he
was greatly admired by
his fellow citizens for
having discovered a
wonderful innovation on
changing a diaper.
—Damon Runyon

THEY TAKE BATHS

„RAKO"

Le Bain des Bébés

REX
2175

Even when
freshly washed
and relieved of
all obvious
confections,
children tend
to be sticky.
—Fran Lebowitz

have one. —Leo Burke

People who say they sleep like a baby usually don't

38

THE BABY should go to sleep promptly when put to bed and should not expect to be rocked or have lullabies sung to him.

—Dr. Herman N. Bundesen

FOREIGN

2 CENTS

281

OFF TO BED.

ANGELS WHOSE WINGS DECREASE
AS THEIR LEGS INCREASE

Alienated Spirits

A trick that

everyone abhors

In little girls is

slamming doors.

—Hilaire Belloc

"Isn't it a
        funny thing,
Mary Poppins,"
        he said
drowsily. "I've
        been so very
naughty and I
        feel so very
good."
        —P. L. Travers

Keep a good-sized waste-paper basket in the nursery. Teach the children to throw into it the bits of paper and other refuse of their play hours. It will give them the habit of neatness and cleanliness without an effort, and save much unnecessary work for the mother. —*The New Century Home Book*

Woe to the land that's governed by a child!

William Shakespeare

"I don't want ever
to be a man,"
he said with passion.
"I want always
to be a little boy
and to have fun."

—J. M. Barrie

We all of us wanted babies—but did we want children? / Either than • for all other countries.